# SOME ANIMAL

Design and typesetting by Mary Austin Speaker
Text set in Jenson
Cover art: "Two-Headed *Lampropeltis gentulus californiae*"
© Arizona Board of Regents / ASU Ask A Biologist

Cataloging-in-publication data is available from the Library of Congress

Nightboat Books
New York
www.nightboat.org

# SOME ANIMAL

Ely Shipley

NIGHTBOAT BOOKS
NEW YORK

# Table of Contents

# PLAYING DEAD

Tiresias had once struck with his staff
two huge snakes as they mated in the forest;
for that, he had been changed—a thing of wonder—

—Ovid, Book III of *The Metamorphoses*


Inversion…is found more commonly in young subjects,
tending to become less marked, or to die out, after puberty.

—Havelock Ellis, *Sexual Inversion*

When from this wreathed tomb shall I awake!
When move in a sweet body fit for life,
And love, and pleasure, and the ruddy strife
Of hearts and lips! Ah, miserable me!

—John Keats, *Lamia*

… a tighter breathing,
And zero at the bone.

—Emily Dickinson, "A Narrow Fellow"

O, lift me …

I fall …

—Percy Bysshe Shelley, "Ode To The West Wind"

I climb the old junior high fence to sit with friends
beneath a tree between baseball fields. Each of us places
a piece of confetti-like paper, carefully unwrapped
from foil onto our tongues. D. says, *this piece is part of a rose.*
Nothing happens. Think: *it's all a joke. Placebo. No such thing.*
*It's all inside a person's mind.*

But still, we wait. We want to see.

I'm fourteen with a red petal on my tongue. I want
to see—I'm not sure what—a miracle.

In 7th grade, Phys. Ed. becomes Sex Ed. for a few weeks.
My classroom a trailer parked in a row of other trailers
at the edge of a basketball court. My teacher stands
at the front of the warm carpeted box. I sit in back, closest
to the door. He is surrounded by sections,

orchestra-like seating.

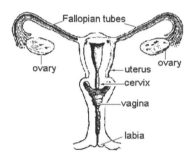

On the overhead projector, a diagram.

The classroom quiet. Rapt. Wrapped in gauze. No one speaks, no
one jokes, though the teacher smiles, says, *one way to remember this for
the test is that it looks like a ram's head.*

I see

the luminous animal skull. A sun
bleaching from inside a desert
of quiet. My mouth

gauze and cotton. My breath
shallow. My head now at rest
on the desk. The face of the beast

aglow beneath my lids, a voice
through mist, O
*what can ail thee....*

The voice of a classmate sharpens into focus: *Are you okay?*
*I see a lily on thy brow*
*With anguish moist and fever dew,*
*And on thy cheeks a fading rose*
*Fast withereth too.*

I see the animal skull superimposed on my classmate's face. I lift my
head to mutter, *Think I'm gonna to be sick*, hear someone cry out, *She*
*needs the nurse!*

With pink hall pass in my moist palm, I amble
down the classroom ramp
    on stilt-like legs, the green stalks of bamboo that
    grew in the backyard. They didn't break
    easily, but bended and bended.
    I'd make flutes, or spin one quick overhead.

    A hollow hole makes a black whirring, whistling
    sound. All there is

    to hear now. Helicopter
    in the black sky.

    White light everywhere. A blinding
    electric trace. The bamboo briefly
    a boat. I float on it, until it, too, disappears.

    Black lake a vibration. Cool
    pavement beneath my cheek. My face
    sails. My face mirrored in sails. Sails
    that petal atop the lake's skin. My face
    on the face of the lake. Beads of

sweat, ice spiders crawl into my hip
crease, along my forehead, the back of
my neck. Shadows close in, blur near.
Somehow, I know

they're there.

*Is she dead?* They ask.    *Oh
God.*    Says a voice,

    *That girl just fell.*

        *That's not a girl, that's a boy.*

    *Oh.    No, wait:    what is it?*

        *A girl.    Someone
get help!*

I can't speak, as if paralyzed.

Sometime near puberty, I begin to experience episodes
of Sleep Paralysis (SP).

> In some cases…people feel that someone is in the room
> with them, some experience the feeling that someone or
> something is sitting on their chest … they feel impending
> death and suffocation.

In folkloric accounts, people believed a demon, ghost, the Old Hag,
also known as a night-mare, sat on the victim's ribs.

When I report my experiences to my best friend, J. tells me

*It's the devil sitting on your chest. It's a sign*
*from God: you need to change your sinful ways.*

   *What sinful ways?*

*No one but you and God know.*

   *Oh.*

[Because] personal accounts of night-mare attacks are not widely shared, enormous relief comes with the realization that others recognize one's experience.

The next time I experience SP, I hear a hissing sound that seems to whisper, whistle, whir, *Satan, sssss, Satan, sssss.* A snake slithers in. In and out of my body, the sound presses. *Shhh. Shhhh.*

But I can't move out from under the weight of my own body that stays asleep, stuffed with gauze I can't even move my mouth to scream for help.

Hysteria, once thought to be a mental illness particular to women, derives from the Greek "hystera," which translates as "uterus."

Plato describes the womb as animal…a living creature desiring union, which, if it remains unfruitful … beyond its proper season, travels around the body blocking passages, obstructing breathing, and causing diseases….

Aretaeus …. describes the womb as… 'like some animal inside an animal … like a living thing inside another living thing.'

I dream I'm beneath the enormous mulberry tree near a childhood
playground, wading fully clothed, in a half empty pool.
I know I once sat here, near these swings, to collect
this mulberry tree's leaves, to later watch in class
silkworms, caged in glass, eat them.

I'm a teenager. The swings hang. And hardly
breathe. I'm all alone inside

a riddle. Leaves drift down from sky, float on the pool's surface.
Both overcast. Some leaves have dried and scrape along nearby
concrete. Thunder cracks and rain falls into the pool. Dread
crawls over me. Lead in my limbs. As if the drain is sucking me
down into it. Something larger and heavier than water or leaves
rains down now. Something emerges
from the deep.

Pale bodies in S shapes slither and glide, slick over water-skin.
I pull my heavy body toward the steps. My feet scrape
stone. I picture them blister and bleed. Ribbons of red.
My body drained of movement. The red water might
drown me.

Large albino snakes swim toward me. White roots dangle.
Some coil on the lawn at the edge of the pool.
They close in—white scales of light
everywhere until my sight goes black.

*A narrow fellow in the grass*

*His notice sudden is*

In societies in which the night-mare is not widely acknowledged or discussed, its dramatic symptoms are sometimes mistaken for evidence of physical or mental illness.

Just as the ordinary colour-blind person is congenitally insensitive to those red-green rays which are precisely the most impressive to the normal eye, and given an extended value to the other colours—finding that blood is the same colour as grass, and a florid complexion blue as the sky—so the invert fails to see emotional values patent to normal persons, transferring their values to emotional associations which for the rest of the world are utterly distinct. Or

we may compare inversion to such a phenomenon as coloured-hearing in which there is not so much defect, as an abnormality of nervous tracks producing new and involuntary combinations. Just as the colour-hearer instinctively associates colour with sounds, like the Japanese lady who remarked when listening to singing,

"That boy's voice is red!"

I wake with an upset stomach when I'm eleven, amble

to the bathroom, sit sleepily on the toilet. I glance down,

dark red blood, nearly a brown, in my underwear. The world blurs.

Everything white light, then electric imprint of the bathroom tile

when I shut my eyes. Paisley patterns swim around one another in

circles, then ricochet into squares. Lightning box. I shut my eyes

again. Breath shallow, I sweat. I yell,

*Mom, come quick. I'm bleeding!*

[Pyramus] picks up Thisbe's veil, and carries it with him to the shadow of the tree they had chosen. Kissing the token, and wetting it with tears, he cries, "Now, be soaked in my blood too." Having spoken he drove the sword he had been wearing into his groin, and, dying, pulled it, warm, from the wound. As he lay back again on the ground, the blood spurted out, like a pipe fracturing at a weak spot in the lead, sending long bursts of water hissing through the split, cutting through the air, beat by beat. Sprinkled with blood, the tree's fruit turned a deep blackish-red, and the roots, soaked through, also imbued the same overhanging mulberries with the dark purplish colour.

She rushes in and lies my sweating body down on the cool
linoleum floor. Underwear, a dressing, manacled around the ankles.
*Take deep breaths. I'll get you a Maxi pad and clean panties.*

Panties. Maxi pad. Her voice static along my skin. I shudder, cold
in my sweat. I hear her close the door, then yell— to whom?
my dad, brother, sister, the neighbors?

*—We have a little woman in the house!*

Humans have a *natural* fear of
blood and injury. Discomfort, nausea,
[hormone regulation] changes,
lightheadedness, and feeling faint

are not unusual in the *normal* population
… Human fainting …

may be a trait evolved
from the tonic immobility or 'playing dead'
observed in many animal species
when confronted with specific fears.

.…'emotional fainting' could be
a physiological activation of a specific
evolutionary reflex rather than an acquired
cultural phenomenon.

*normal* (adj)
standing at a right angle


*scared stiff* (idiom)
extremely frightened


*Jill awoke from a dream that left her afraid—scared stiff, in fact.*


Etymology: from the idea that you are *stiff (unable to bend or change your position)* because you are too frightened to move

I skateboard all morning, but eventually have to come home to use the bathroom. I think of my friends, boys, using bushes near the playground, or climbing the fence to get onto the roof of the school's cafeteria and aim onto trees below.
I skate several blocks to go alone.

The bathroom is dark when I enter. Only light from the doorway illuminates me from the side, all shadow and wild long hair.

the Bloody Mary ritual is a prepubescent
fantasy about the imminent onset of menses
To summon the ghost,

the girls go into the bathroom
where they prick their fingers with a pin
to draw a drop of blood.

The 'flowing' of blood from their bodies
induces a young pale-faced girl
to appear in the mirror
"blood running down her face
from a large cut in her forehead"

an instance of "upwards displacement"
blood issuing from the head
instead of from the urinogenital area

substantiated by the historical
relationship between the words

'maidenhood' and 'maidenhead' …

the assignment of facial features
to the vagina, e.g., as mouth with lips (labia)

which confirms the symbolic
equivalence of head and genital area.

My Metallica shirt clings to my chest with sweat when I flip on the light. Bud-like shapes just beneath the band's insignia, bud-like horns just above a skull. I peel back the skull to see.

The nipples have changed from small dime shapes to oblong eyes. They stare and seem sad. I grab the small lumps in my fists. I try to crush away the alien crowns. But can't. They're red and swollen. They're bigger now. A wave of nausea tilts me. I don't faint, but move to the toilet to puke. Can't.

Before heading out I put another shirt on under Metallica, even though it's early August in Southern California and somewhere near 100 degrees.

# ARRAY OF UFO SHAPES

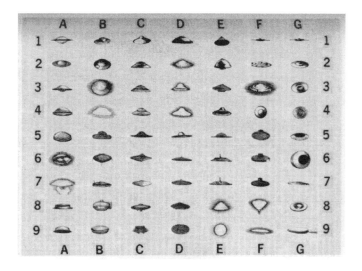

In other reports of SP, the victim or abductee awakens from sleep with a feeling of dread or a sense of a presence in the room. The bedroom may be flooded with light that is often accompanied by a buzzing or humming sound. The aliens either come to get the abductee or the victim is transported or 'floated' to a spacecraft. Once inside the craft, the person may be subjected to various medical procedures that typically involve the removal of eggs or sperm...The human victim feels helpless and is often restrained or partially or completely paralyzed during the encounter.

I visit my friend H., who has escaped to college in another city. I sneak into her sexuality course. A large screen projects photographs of vagina after vagina to an audience of hundreds. Each time a new vagina appears on the screen the light in the auditorium changes. The flesh color beams down and cascades over the heads and shoulders of the onlookers.

When the vagina with a speculum clamping it open appears, I see the cervix. Red alien crown. My skull splits and I float up into a misty light through the vaginal colors. The speculum's metal blinds me in seconds. It gleams to a white hum.

I feel each half of my skull hum in my teeth. I fumble
to hands and knees and crawl to the classroom door.
Just outside, I can't move; on the cool linoleum floor, I lay
down my sweating body.

By sophomore year, my inability to make eye contact with anyone has only gotten worse. I keep my head down, get my work done, talk to no one. I take easy electives to keep up my GPA, though I have some interest in one class that has something to do with psychology. There is a whole unit on child development and birth. We watch a film from the early 80s. Its trippy music reminds me of *Close Encounters of the Third Kind*.

The classroom is dark, except for what looks like a 60s liquid light show projected onto the screen. It reminds me of M.'s lava lamp and my dad's Iron Butterfly album *In a gadda da vida*. My dad once told me that when the band recorded the song they were too high to say "In the garden of Eden" clearly, and so it became this distortion. I have the song in my head for the rest of the film, a happier sound than the movie's eerie, but still psychedelic synthesizers that drift beneath the narrator's voice, charting the journey of the sperm swimming up to penetrate the egg.

One slithers in, gets swallowed. I'm surprised I've made it this far without fainting. Maybe I can stomach it because it looks more like a documentary on the deep sea or outer space. Maybe the spells were a phase.

I'm only vaguely nauseous when from behind a boy whispers: *I can smell it. You on your rag? Yeah, you must be. I can smell it. You must be bleeding right now. I'd fuck it anyway—stir some soup, make babies.*

He whispers loud enough for everyone sitting near to hear. They giggle, but the laughter is jagged. He whispers loud enough, but not so loud that the teacher can make out the words. She shushes the back corner of the room where I've been assigned to sit. *Shhhh, shhhh.*

He waits, then starts in again. This time they stay quiet. Maybe they're scared of getting into trouble. Or they're just as scared of him as I am. Telling only makes things worse. I'm already picked on enough, and he's already been sent to the dean's office, even suspended a few times. There are rumors about why. Something about a fight. Was there a knife?

I can feel the heat of him against me, his heavy breath at the back of my head. I recall him coming into class. White t-shirt. Blue jeans. Clean cut. But he smells oily. Not like oily skin, but more like the oil from an engine, a garage. Is it because he's just come from shop? Is it the way his home smells? I try to imagine his home. It's dark. I think, his family is not nice to him, or his family is never home. I think, this boy is as lonely as me. I wonder why I'm able to keep mine on the inside, why I have to. Why is it bursting out of him? Why is he so mean? Maybe this is what all teen boys smell like when they are angry and lonely. He says he can smell me. I begin to believe maybe he can.

Next class, a woman from a local hospital visits to explain childbirth and answer our questions about the movie. She's helped to deliver babies before. She tells us, *You'd think the work would be done after the baby comes out! But then there's the third phase: the placenta and membranes.* And, *It can be very bloody, as the placenta tears away from the uterus.*

The room fades. The woman only a shape, silver outline, shimmer against the blackboard. The room tilts into a two dimensional plane of dark. I lift my body, float toward the teacher. I know I can't collapse here. I don't want them to whisper or laugh over my stunned body. I have to get away from the boy who smells of oil. Everything is smudged with smoke. I try not to get swallowed up, try not to choke.

I hold the back of each chair for balance. The teacher's face looms near, an aura. I'm sure I've gone pale when I manage to mutter: *I need to step out for air.* Outside, I rest on the cool concrete step. At first, I only allow myself to sit and lean back against the door. I want to lie down. Drenched in sweat, I take deep breaths. My mind whirls. I see ghost-like spirals, snake-like smoke.

I hide in the library before and after school. I hide
until nearly everyone has gone.
I read about witches that straddle broomsticks
slathered with ointment that makes them fly—
       the vulgar believe, and the witches confess
       they anoint a staff and ride on it
       anoint themselves
       under arms and in other hairy places
       and sometimes carry
       charms under their hair.
I read of ointment made from *Datura*
       also known as the devil's
       apple, thorn apple, mad
       apple, the devil's weed, Gabriel's
       trumpet, and angel's trumpet.
I read of potions made from
       mandrake, henbane, or belladonna,
       deadly nightshade.
I read that the bark of the white mulberry is an antidote
to the venom of certain snakes.

Now, the sky brightens over the junior high school baseball fields, and the sound of the airplane, arrowing across sky, slices my body into slow echoes. Blades of grass, grown into emeralds, now jet up and through D.'s pale paper doll face. A mirror. His eyes shoot emerald spears through their sockets. He's laughing and I'm frightened, then enormously happy. I feel now as if forever near tears. My body purls out from itself, as if out from his eyes.

When we reach the street we fear the speed and sound of passing cars. Rockets. Crashing waves. The sound makes our skin ache. We walk along together, arm-in-arm, one big beast.

We walk all the way across town to a fast food chain to buy 90c
sodas with free refills. I can't take my eyes off the grain in the table's
wood. It moves in endless ocean waves, until my forearm begins
to pulse and heave, breaking out in tattoos that move. A snake, its
scales pulse

> *Vermilion-spotted, golden, green, and blue;*
> *Striped like a zebra, freckled like a pard,*
> *Eyed like a peacock, and all crimson barr'd;*
> *And full of silver moons, that, as [I] breathed,*
> *Dissolv'd, or brighter shone, or interwreathed*
> *Their lustres with the gloomier tapestries—*
> *So rainbow-sided, touch'd with miseries*

At first I'm frightened, but the snake emanates benevolence. I show
my friends. They see it too.

> *a whip lash,*
> *unbraiding in the sun.*

When I look at their faces I see more tattoos. Blossoms
from their skins in the softest colors I've ever seen. Feathers
of fledglings.

We walk to the grocery store. Fruits and vegetables radiate
their colors. They hum. I caress the red cabbage head, in love with
its velvet swirl, a tide of
violet I feel moving through me.

*head and lyre*

*a miracle!*

Here,


as the head lay exposed on the alien sand, its moist
hair dripping brine, a fierce snake attacked it. But at last
Phoebus came…and turned the serpent's gaping jaws to
stone, [freezing] the mouth, wide open, as it was.

Four, maybe five-years old, in the empty garage that smelled of oil, I capture, in a bucket, a lizard, large as my forearm. With no escape, its tiny nails scratch the metal. It scurries in circles. My kid hands in garden gloves reach in, grip between head and neck, so it can't move to bite me, just like my dad taught me if ever I had to catch a snake. My other hand, dwarfed in the garden glove, holds its tail. I pull and pull, until I see a line of blood ooze out from a pattern in his scales.

I'm surprised. Up to then, the image had been cartoon. I wanted simply to see the tail that was supposed to grow back in place of the one I'd pull away.

I am overcome by blood, my face flushed. My mom appears at my side, takes the bucket, and flings the lizard out into the yard. I see its body in a flash, scrawny skeleton against the sun. I am full of blood, dizzy with it. The blood light takes my breath.

I drown in blood. The door to the world outside the dark garage is contained in a square of light, but the square tilts, the square leading to the backyard, the dying grass in the summer lawn—where my mother stands, scolding me—and the lizard scurrying into the woodpile. Tinged, the seam at the dark of the garage door and the light of the world outside is red.

Beneath the pine, the blond
neighbor boy, a teen
in a bathrobe, bare
foot and tip toeing

over pinecones, slipped it through
the slit of the chain link fence.
*Touch it. Touch it.*
*Don't be afraid.*

What is it?
*It's okay. Don't be afraid.*

He had pet snakes, mice
to feed them, or was it
one of the new born kittens

curled in his palm
little breaths heaving it
to life? Then his voice, *please*

*please don't tell.*

Days, maybe weeks later, I play near the woodpile. My paper plane crash lands near the chain link fence. Near the crumpled paper wings, I see the body of the lizard, shriveled and black.

As I lift my arm to stroke the head again, M. seizes my hand

*You're acting crazy; someone will see. We could get caught.*

The biomedical premise that direct spiritual experiences are psychopathological, as well as the mainstream religious view that they are heretical, suppresses the reporting and discussing of nightmare encounters.

We end in the safety of M.'s room. The singer's voice helicopters
from one corner to another, encircling us. His voice parachutes
down, sings *a resurrection…* The sound of the bass appears
over us, a great black drop, pulsing and leaking
from the center of the ceiling. I'm afraid it'll fall. I want it to.
Together we bathe in the big black notes. *I've got some friends*

*inside…* I glimpse myself in the mirror. I've been warned
never to stare in a mirror while here. Don't even ask why, just do it
anyway. My gaze a gaping question. Pupils an abyss. The center of
an inverse universe, eternal corridor of mirror reflecting deeper
into some ancient beginning that is also an always and impossible
future staring back. Mouth of a hungry ghost. Narcissus. Bloody

Mary. I want to see—I'm not sure what. Stare hard
to hear, its music clear: maiden in a meadow, faery
creature. Her garlands coil around her
crown. Her body blooms into
flowers. Blossoms from her eyes
and breasts, roots and vines down her
torso and legs. She is a tree that begins
to age. Her bark, more cavernous, molts. Leaves
fall away. Skin wilts from her face. Buds

retract. I see myself a shadow, alone
and cradling the luminous
animal skull. The shade

tears and weaves
long grey strands of hair

between the skull's horns. One blurred hand
strums the space between. A black lake

of vibration. The sky behind. A gauze
of cloud. I see the music's soft
distortion, bleaching wisps

flutter there, dissolve
in winds of guitars.

# A SWEET TEEN

Isolation on a flimsy mattress. Floating out
in books and photographs
sheet music for guitar.

Out on the lawn facing the street, the neighbors
are strangers. The mailman comes but she never sees him. The mail
truck creeps by   a cloud gleaming   to melt in sun. Perhaps
that was a dream too.

\*


The large teenage boy, who looked like a man,
pinned her down
in the dark house when no one else was home.
The one with the long beard that pressed into the soft space
in her clavicle.

\*


An evening curtain billows
over my bed, feathery

owl body. Hover here, over mine. He sinks

his claw in my flesh, locks into bone

above my breast. Clavicle a branch,

a wind instrument. He lifts me. We drift

out over a city. I am naked except for ribbons

of blood that stream from my torso and arms, one

long drop falling



on the forehead

of a girl below

on her way to school.

She furrows her brow,

looks into cloud

sky, reaches for



her umbrella.

She's forgotten it.



*



He was the one who told her there was no such thing

as soul. She knew there was because she saw

her grandmother dead at the wake. She could tell her soul had left

her body. Just a mask, waxy and flat.
He laughed at her and said
her grandmother looked flat because they had taken her insides out
and embalmed her. He laughed and he laughed.

\*


He eats the soft parts first,
eyes and tongue. My face becomes
cave before he lies me down
in a field of tall grass and wild

flowers. My bones
hum bright in sun.

\*


At the cemetery she had seen a group of people
dressed in white, angels picnicking
on the long green summer lawn.

One day he came over in his red Mustang, blasting Patsy Cline.
The music was hazy. The leaves in the wind swayed and
made the light gold. He brought her a 35c ice cream cone
from Thrifties. Sweet enough to make her sick.

He was big boned with long blond hair
and a red beard. She could never remember
the color of his eyes. She tried not to look into them. His mouth
was thin, his nose small. He was pale, freckled, and doughy.
She did not like him. He kept pressing into her though
he rarely touched her.
She would not let him. Everywhere she went
she thought he might be watching.

*

He had a tattoo but she could never remember it. His mother
was never home. Or his mother was drunk in a distant bedroom.

Sometimes a man was with his mother. She could hear
them murmuring through the walls. The windows always
closed. Dark and warm. Quiet. Still as a swampy puddle.

*

One day he dyed his long beard a darker red. His friends made fun
of him. They said he had a bloody tampon hanging from his chin.
Grotesque. A purple ring
in his eyebrow. And a tattoo she can't remember.

*

One day he came to her room and saw pictures
she was drawing of teenage boys who looked just like her except
they were boys. They played music
and rode skateboards just like her. They wore black t-shirts and
tight ripped jeans just like her. They had tattoos

and piercings and hair as long as or longer than hers. Sometimes
she named them and she loved their names, Michael, Elijah,
Jonathan, Jonathan, and Noah. She never told anyone their names.
He noted the pronounced bulges between their thighs, and
called her pervert.


At night she would become the boys she drew,
and replay her whole day as if she were
a boy. She felt easy and happy in her boring life that way, riding
her skateboard on the half-pipe she had built.
She coasted along each side and then up into air. She
was suspended there. Sometimes she turned in circles slowly across
the sky until the wheels caught the wood again and she coasted up
the other side, smooth and firm, until she lifted up again into
the sky, her long hair turning all around her, white sun spiraling
everywhere. Sometimes she gazed down to see her calf covered in
downy hair and watched her strong muscles tilting
the board to float a little higher as if she could surf sky.
Or she'd see her thickening hand grip the edge of the ramp
so that she could plant herself there in a hand stand, feet high

in the sky above her, the board in her other hand
and her sternum filling with the white sunlight she was opening and
opening.

Finally, she would retire into a door she had built
into the side of the ramp. She had made a home of it.

*

In her dream there was nothing left to dream. There was only being.
She was invisible at school. No one
staring, especially not him.

*

Inside a cave for nine years, we sleep
for the first time in the seventh and wake

angry. With a knife I slice
each eye lid. Soft as newborn's

foreskin. Where our fallen flesh
touches earth, tea trees blossom.

*

There had been a glass rosary around her grandmother's
hands, thin as parchment, sleeping inside the white coffin. Her
skin is pulled down by earth. Her face pulled into a grimace. Grave
face. She wants to say, don't worry. Now, she is entering earth, her
grandmother's glass rosary coiling around the whitening bones.

*

Canyon the color of ash.
We kneel beside a stream.
Here, water is silver
and reflects sky. Blue with white streaks
of cloud. Somewhere nearby something
moves through the milky water. Now,
we're submerged. A small pale octopus
hovers. Its tentacles tusk-
like, snake-like, a medusa
head. Because we're afraid
we rise away. I turn to see
the silver stream

disappear. A slender snake
swims toward us. We part a little
to let it pass. The sky is bright between us.

\*

It was the summer she lay in front of the amplifier
she'd connected to her record player.
She listened to an old album she'd stolen
from her grandparents. She lay on the ocean
blue carpet. She let the sound wash
over her. She came
without touching herself.

\*

It was the summer she threw herself onto her mattress
and looked up at the print of
Monet's water lilies
hanging above, and broke

through the wall to float in the warm
water of the paint. She could breathe inside it
and thought of Ophelia who never really
seemed dead. They were not dead in the water. She was not
suffocating with a mouth painted shut

painted into a square
of blue hung on the wall
of a teenage girl.

# ON BATHROOMS

A train arrives at a station. A little boy and a little girl, brother and sister, are seated in a compartment face to face next to the window through which the buildings along the station platform can be seen passing as the train pulls to a stop. "Look," says the brother, "We're at Ladies!" "Imbecile!" replies his sister, "Can't you see we're at Gentlemen?".... For these children, Ladies and Gentlemen will be henceforth two countries toward which each of their souls will strive on divergent wings.

–Jacques Lacan, "The Instance of the Letter in the Unconscious"

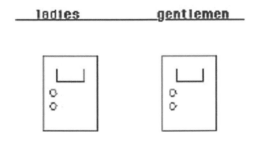

1.

During recess, she enters the girls' bathroom, notes the older girls around the mirror—more of them than she expects—drops her eyes, slips past them as quickly as she can into a free stall. She hopes they don't see her. But they do.

She squats but can't relieve herself. The tiles are fake green marble, the stall door beige. She suppresses a sigh. She cannot go until the voices quiet too. Are they still there? Her bladder opens. Her warm stream fills the bowl, until the door opens.

Before she can look up, in one thrust she manages to pull up her pants, slam the door wide, and fly into the frail body of the small dirty girl her age, who wears the same clothes every day. She grabs the front of her shirt, a soft flower print with a lace collar. She lifts her from the ground and presses her into the awful green marble wall.

*Don't you ever, Don't you ever,* she heaves through her clenched chest. The small dirty girl begins to cry, *I'm sorry, I'm sorry I didn't mean to I'm sorry.* She feels her hot breath on her knuckles through the thin slit of her tensed mouth. The girl quivers.

Now what? She can't hit her. She can't go further. She turns to the mirror where the crowd of older girls—the same ones?—gawk.

She wants to hit them. She will hit the girl in order to hit them, make them wince in pain, look away.

They threaten. *We're telling! You'd better stop. We're going to tell that you're beating up Angela!* Angela, the other kid everyone makes fun of, comes to school with dirt and grass in her hair. She wears the same blouse with the flower print and lace collar every day, smells like woods.

But then it comes. Angela is a girl. They all want to know. *Why are you in the girls' bathroom? You're in the wrong room. Why don't you go to the boys' room?*

Earlier that year, the boy from India, who wears a blue suit to school every day, is walking in from the playground, in from recess, after the bell to line up has rung. He walks into the gymnastic bars, cuts his skull open. Blood trickles down his white shirt, his blue suit, and he falls backward into the playground sand. She wants to run to him to help, but doesn't know how. She can't move. It's quicksand, a slow motion movie; she sinks with him.

Why cast this sun on the blacktop in the middle of the day on the playground? Why did the Indian boy in the blue suit simply walk into the bar? Why has he fallen? Why are they no longer in the green grass with the great white parachute, running beneath it, crouching down while it billows its great cloud body over them? Why are they not laughing together beneath the white sheet in the shady grass at the center of a world somewhere far from here? Why has he fallen at the periphery? Why must he bleed everywhere in the sand all over his white shirt and his blue suit while the teachers run toward him, crowd around, send someone for help?

He lies in the sand, blood in his hair, and stares blankly up into the sun. The white of his eyes, the white of the parachute in the field shivers.

One walks in a daydream and walks into objects and what does one feel? The pain of anything at all? The outside trying to get in while one's insides seep out into the playground?

She wants to make the girls bleed. She wants to tear into them. She wants to bash their foreheads. She looks into the light brown eyes flecked with red. The dirty girl's chin quivers. Her breath soft, pants against her face, pleading.

The boy doesn't return to class that day. The next, he wears a bandage, stitches, waxy wires sprouting out from beneath his hair. Frankenstein's monster from a foreign country, wears strange clothes, doesn't speak their language, no one plays with him or knows his name.

2.

The bell rang, signaling the time to line up
*It was clear that it was my turn*[1]

I lay in the sand with blood in my hair
*peacefully*   I stared blankly up

*He asked what "I had*
*down there"*

*She patted me down*
skull cut open

*and proceeded to refer to me as "she"*
You're in the wrong

*room with 2 cells and a bathroom.*
the awful green marble

You're in the wrong.

---

1    Justin Adkins, "Police Mistreatment of a Transgender Man--Brooklyn
     Bridge Occupy Wall Street Protest Saturday, October 3rd, 2011, 1:39pm,"
     justinadkins.com

arrested for a variety of crimes,
some violent. I can't move. handcuffed
my right wrist to a metal handrail. Quicksand,
I remained

handcuffed to this bar
next to the bathroom for the next 8 hours.

every person had to use the toilet
next to where they had me
locked to the railing.

The smell of urine was so strong
It billowed

over me    She turned my chair
my arm still locked to the railing but now pinned behind my back.

I wore a bandage.
they were bringing in women to use the restroom
and she could not have me watching.

I wore strange clothes.
*outside the glass wall*   my cut skull

see the stitches
*a laugh*

*curious and freakish*   wires
beneath my hair   the white of
my eyes

*the officers laughed even more*
One feels the outside trying to get in

send someone for help   *I needed*
*to urinate*   *I was in danger*   the white of

the parachute in the field
shivered

# ON BEARDS:

# A MEMOIR OF PASSING

I am large, I contain multitudes.

—Walt Whitman, "Song of Myself"

Where are we going, Walt Whitman? The doors close in
an hour. Which way does your beard point tonight?

—Allen Ginsberg, "Supermarket in California"

Ni un solo momento, viejo hermoso Walt Whitman,
he dejado de ver tu barba llena de mariposas ...

—Federico Garcia Lorca, "Oda a Walt Whitman"

I dip my fingers into an amber colored ashtray
beside my parents' bed, move to the mirror

where my father shaves each morning,
lift my fingers to my face, and smear
dark ash above my lip, and across my chin, rub

until it's sea green.

I'm a pirate. I grip my dagger,
a piece of cardboard wrapped in tin foil. It shimmers

over my beard.

*

Ancient Egyptians and Romans let their beards and hair grow out
when grieving. Conversely, Greeks shaved and cut theirs.
This may have evolved into the ritual of 18th century English
widows covering or even cutting

their hair after a husband's death.

To lose my other is to lose my self.

*

When she becomes he, people are confused, some are even angry.
For example, his girlfriend's mother

gets so flustered one day, "she, I mean, he, oh…" she
begins to call him "it."

He's been called it before—

*

In seventh grade first period math she slumps forward in her seat, hides
behind the hair she's been growing. It's a tent that whispers
against the back of her

thighs when she walks. The teacher never calls on her. She
never raises her hand. She is safe. No one ever asked Cousin It, what

are you, a boy or a girl?

She is reluctant to change into her gym clothes. Most days she sneaks into the stall to change, even though it's forbidden. The coaches linger at the edge of the bathroom, watch for shorts sliding down over sneakers, pooling on the floor. On the toilet seat, she balances carefully. A circus act for an acrobat, a bearded lady.

\*

A portrait reveals eighteen-year-old Annie Jones, one of P.T. Barnum's bearded ladies, hair pulled back and tied by a black ribbon. Her face is fully exposed, though more than half of it is covered by her enormous beard and thick dark eyebrows. She wears a long fur coat that reaches her knees, where a dress adorned with large flowers flares out, then ends at the bottom, a ruffle along the seam. The fur coat looks less like fur and more like the long wavy tresses of a mane, an extension of her hair and beard. She is nearly completely covered in hair, except for her shadowy eyes which look to her side, into distance, the field of her flowery dress. Her thin fingers rest delicately together over a long piece of fabric broadening out from behind her.

With few exceptions, facial hair on women has been the object of
neglect and scorn.

No historic edicts, laws, or papal decrees have ever governed its growth.

When St Kummernus' father ("kummer" meaning sorrow) sought
to marry her off
to a neighboring heathen,
she grew a beard, a visible sign
she belonged exclusively to God.
Her furious father

had her killed.

\*

Hair does not continue to grow after death. Tissues
around it (especially on the face) contract and expose it,
giving the dead their five o'clock shadow.

The grandchild plays on the porch
with a toy gun, long blond hair flaring out
like a halo. The grandchild refuses to shoot
the grandfather, a transsexual, tells him, "You're the good
monster, grandpa! Yes, the good monster."[1]

*

I sit in a parked car with my grandma, while my mom buys gas.
"Where we going, Grandma?" She says, "To buy pretty dresses
for your first day of school." An anchor ratchets down in me.
"I don't want to wear a dress!" She raises her voice,

"Girls wear dresses
and you're going to wear one
whether you like it or not."

The car feels like a great balloon
expanding. The air around my face
swells with red mute yells
from within. Waves of heat rise
from the balloon's elastic skin.

---

1  Scene from the documentary *Southern Comfort.*

I too yell: "I'm a boy! A boy."

It's the first time I have ever said this to anyone.

Grandma lets out a long sigh, "Well then, if you're a boy,

let's see your penis."

*

*Abak he stirte, and thoughte it was amys,*

*For wel he wiste a womman hath no berd.*[2]

---

2    From Chaucer's *The Miller's Tale.*

*FTM candidates actually practice the narrative of gender essentialism*
*they are required to perform before they go in to see the doctors*
*…the price of using the diagnosis to get what one wants…*
*one cannot use language to say what one really thinks is true*

*One pays for one's freedom*
*as it were*
*by sacrificing one's claim to use language*
*truthfully*

—Judith Butler, from *Undoing Gender*

*A berd! A berd!*[3]

*

We are painting pictures.

I have stacks of paper, and even a roll of butcher paper at home.
Drawing is what I love to do most. I draw what I have called
since I could speak, "mens," two-dimensional, flat pictures of
older boys doing all sorts of things I do or want to do—
play baseball, play drums, be in a club or even a gang, skateboard.

When I draw I'm in another world.

Painting is different. The water colors move
out of my control. I've already dripped a fat black drop
onto my self-portrait. I begin to move
the brush along the jaw line in the papery mirror. I spread
the thick mistake into a beard.

---

3    Ibid.  In Middle English, "berd" can mean both facial hair and trick.

Mrs. Hertz passes my table and pauses, "Oh look!
How wonderful! That must be Abraham Lincoln. Is that
Abraham Lincoln? Look children,　　　　　　is painting
one of our most important presidents!" I am the shyest
student in class. I never speak. The kids will laugh.

I like the way my face looks out at me
through its beard. I keep my eyes on my face,
nod my head, and begin to paint a long line across its forehead.

A dark cloudy frown will become
a stove top hat. He will need more than a beard
if he is really going to be Abraham Lincoln.

After recess, we spread out around the room
to hang the dry paintings. Mrs. Hertz gets the teacher next door
so that she can admire our work. The other teacher immediately expresses
how impressed she is with the picture
of Abraham Lincoln.

I am sent to the principal's office for the first time, where
everyone smiles at me and Abraham Lincoln.
"What a lovely painting" and
"aren't you so pretty!" I believe I am
a great artist.

A few weeks later, at open house, my parents and I arrive to find
Abraham Lincoln wearing a long and shiny blue ribbon. He has won
first prize for the annual district contest. Everyone is smiling
except Abraham Lincoln. I look at him. He stares through me.

*

> *Axis IV:*  *Problems Related to the Social Environment: Difficulty
> being accepted in social environment due to incongruence
> between expressing masculinity and lack of masculine
> physical attributes.*

(From letter from therapist to endocrinologist and sex reassignment
surgeon in accordance with the Harry Benjamin Standards of Care
and the DSM IV.)

One fall, he and his girlfriend go to the movies.
The parking lot is crowded with cars
full of teenagers blaring music. A group of boys calls after them,
"Hey! Hey dykes!" He holds his girlfriend's hand tighter, quickens
his pace, and tries to stare past them. He focuses on his girlfriend's
hand in one of his, and the movie ticket in his other, an aspen leaf
torn from a branch and floating into the cave of his jacket
pocket. They hurry into the safety of the dark theater.
The screen lights up with Brandon Teena's face.


Lana's mom says to him, "Come 'ere and lemme get a look at you."
The audience knows
he is not a "real" man. He's afraid he'll be


discovered. He grips his girlfriend's hand tighter. His breath
quickens. Lana's mom slowly caresses the smooth and hairless skin.
His eyes dart nervously to and from her face. The camera moves
between the mom's face and her hand
on the tense, naked jaw. He is afraid.


At the end of the movie, after the audience has watched
Brandon's rape and beating
for over ten minutes, then how he's shredded

by gun shots, his girlfriend sobs uncontrollably. She buckles
into his arms in a row just behind a path toward the exit.
When the lights come up, people file out. His girlfriend buries
her face in his bound chest.
Strangers stare.

He wants to leave, but is afraid to go out into a dark
parking lot filled with cars
barreling spotlights toward them.

*

*There are two kinds of people in this world that go around beardless—*
*boys and women.*
*I am neither one.*

—Greek saying

*In the context of individual and group therapy,     has expressed his feelings*

*of being male     these feelings*

*surfaced during childhood*

*In addition to his work in therapy,     has also communicated with other female to*

*male transsexuals (FtMs). Being with other F to M individuals,     noted*

*a sense of belonging and comfort*

*he has never experienced*

*in the past. Recently,     made the decision to undergo hormone replacement.*

*Since making this decision, he has noted*

*increased pleasure and an overall sense of "relief."*

(Letter from therapist to endocrinologist and sex reassignment surgeon in accordance with the Harry Benjamin Standards of Care and the DSM IV.)

When he grows out his beard, or what little there is of it, he worries,

Is it full enough? Do I look
like a man? Or a boy

trying to look like a man?

Regardless, he knows that any amount of hair on his face
signifies male.

In a San Francisco bar, a woman slurs
thick through beer breath into his ear,

"I think you're hot"

asks him,

"What's with that?"

pointing to his beard. He tells her,

"I don't know
yet. I'm experimenting."

She says

"You can stop
now; the experiment's

over. It looks
awful, not just awful, but you look
like a twelve-year-old trying
to look tough." *What should I do*

                    *with him? Dress him*
                    *in my apparel*

                    *and make him*
                    *my waiting-gentle*

                    *woman? He that hath a beard*

                    *is more*

                    *than a youth, and he that hath no*

                    *beard is less than a man:*

*and he that is*

*more than a youth*

*is not for me, and he*

*that is less than a man, I am*

*not for him*[4]

The grain in the wall just beyond her head blurs
and swirls. His gaze sinks.

---

4    Shakespeare, *Much Ado About Nothing*.

In gay slang, the word "beard" is used to describe a woman
who is a cover for a gay man's orientation. She, the beard, is used
to hide his identity

by accompanying him in public so that he might pass for straight.

Beards were often "worn"
as a form of protection.

A parallel word, though used less commonly, to describe
a man who appears in society as a cover for a lesbian,
is not a beard, but a "merkin."

A merkin is "an artificial covering of hair for the female pubic region; a pubic
wig for women. Also: an artificial vagina." Merkin is
also slang for "female genitals" (OED).

It's said that a merkin was originally worn by prostitutes
who had to shave their pubic hair when they contracted a disease.

He visits a gynecologist before his hysterectomy, a procedure
transmen are advised to have within the first few years of hormone
replacement therapy because they are at a heightened risk for cancer
in the female reproductive organs. The doctor points at his pelvis,
says, "Don't worry, you won't have to shave all that hair."
Then asks if he wants to see his cervix, tells him, "Take a look.
It's really cool. It looks like you have a penis, a big swollen
penis head."

He looks up and watches the bulbous organ, which seems to float
inside the watery black TV suspended over him and magnifying
everything. It is a planet in a grade school science fair planetarium.
Jupiter angled up as if to breathe. It is a pinkish whale arching its blow hole
out from under the viscous water.

He reminds himself to breathe so that he will not pass out.

*

*farewell*
*with your old dress and a long black beard around the vagina*

—Allen Ginsberg, from "Kaddish"

Some nights he goes to the Otherside,

a piano bar on the east side of Los Angeles that caters to daddies.

When he and another trans friend sit at the bar,

many of the men stare. They cannot be sure of exactly why

the men stare. No one calls them she. No one asks how old,

even though they look fifteen. They are never served drinks

anywhere else without getting carded first,

even though they're nearly thirty.

Usually, when he gets up to go to the restroom, a man will follow.

Once, a man asks, "Are you a model?"

as they stand over the sink washing their hands together. He avoids

looking at the man in the mirror, smiles and focuses on the water,

warm and cascading

over his small hands, and finally says no. Walking back to the bar,

briefly, they make eye contact. The man comes closer to whisper,

"You're just so beautiful."


Another time, a man sitting near him at the bar begins to growl.

The man is dressed in a black leather jacket and black jeans,

wears a full beard. He has his back to the man. He feels

the bone of the man's knee push into his right ass cheek. It jerks

into him a little more each time the man growls. He does not look

at the man, but into his friend's eyes, sucks
in his breath, hesitates, laughs.

*

I am sitting on Santa's lap. I wear a faux fur coat. It is striped black
and white. I am something polar bear and zebra under pig tails. I am

crying. What did I look out and see? A flash of
white light. Spotlight. Lighthouse beam crossing over a drowned
body. And after, a ghost, some dream, thin trace of lightning?

Santa's eyes loom large over his beard. They are brown,
his lashes thick and long, his eyebrows thin
black penciled lines. Face smooth and slight. His beard
is not a part of it. His beard
is a white mask, a shroud. His hands, cold, gloved, a surgeon's.

*

In 16th Century England, a beard was a sign
of sexual virility; the longer the beard, the more potent
the man. Queen Elizabeth I

disliked beards so much she had them taxed.
Men of the clergy usually shaved their beards
to indicate celibacy.

\*

My mom and I sit on the couch and look at old family photos.
We come across one of me on Santa's lap.
"Even though you were so young," she says, "I think you could tell

something wasn't right."

And finally, "That Santa was really a woman."

\*

*In spite of…unaesthetic results transsexual patients…[display]*
*what doctors call a "poor reality" sense …. the patient is regarding his new*
*body theoretically; it is, he is, male, however*
*attractive or unattractive the appearance.*

—Marjorie Garber, from *Vested Interests: Cross-Dressing and*
*Cultural Anxiety*

Under fluorescent lights in a parking lot, his friend looks down
at his chin:
"What
is that?"

He thinks,

tiny seeds sprouting, thin
chain of ants crawling across
my chin, flash of pubic
hair under a gown of—

Instead, says,
"You don't like it? It isn't thick enough yet to grow, is it?"

His friend wags a finger,
"Uh uh, you need to shave that."

A little while later, stopped under the emulsive red glow of traffic lights,
the friend reaches over, grips his thigh, grins,
"Before you shave, can I touch it?"

Pulling the car over, he leans toward his friend, feels his breath

brushing against his cheek. Together they stroke

    a field of

    long grass where

    night blooming

    flowers might

    issue

    from his jaw.

# NOTES

## PLAYING DEAD

Page 3

Book III, "Tiresias," from *The Metamorphoses* by Ovid (translated by Allen Mandelbaum) & *Sexual Inversion* by Havelock Ellis & John Addington Symonds

Page 5

*Lamia* by John Keats & "A narrow fellow in the grass" by Emily Dickinson

Page 7

"Ode to the West Wind" by Percy Bysshe Shelley

Page 11

"La Belle Dame Sans Merci" by John Keats

Page 14

Dement, William C. "Sleep Paralysis." Stanford University. Jan. 1999. Web. Oct. 2017

Pages 16, 22, 34, & 54

Pgs. 27-28, *Sleep Paralysis: Night-mares, Nocebos, and the Mind-Body Connection*, Shelley R. Adler, Rutgers University Press, 2011

Page 18

Pgs. 25-26, "Once Upon a Text: Hysteria from Hippocrates," Helen King, from *Hysteria Beyond Freud*, Sander Gilman, et. al., University of California Press, 1993

Page 21

Dickinson

Page 23

Ellis & Symonds, Pgs. 134-135

Page 25

Book IV, "Pyramus and Thisbe," from *The Metamorphoses* by Ovid (translated by A.S. Kline)

Page 27

Valentina Accurso, MD; Mikolaj Winnicki, MD, PhD; Abu S.M. Shamsuzzaman, MBBS, PhD; Amy Wenzel, PhD; Alan Kim Johnson, PhD; Virend K. Somers, MD, PhD, "Predisposition

to Vasovagal Syncope in Subjects With Blood/Injury Phobia,"
*Circulation*, 2001

Emphasis via italics mine.


Page 28

*Oxford English Dictionary*, 1640s and the *Cambridge Dictionary of Idioms*, 2003


Pages 30-31

Pg.12, Bloody Mary in the Mirror: A Ritual Reflection of Pre-Pubescent Anxiety, Alan Dundes. *Western Folklore*, Vol. 57, No. 2/3 (Spring - Summer, 1998), pp. 119-135


Page 33

"Array of UFO Shapes from Dr. Shephard's proposed witness-interview procedure," 1968 UFO Symposium report, pg. 229


Page 41

Bergamo, Jordanes de, c.1470-71, *Qvaestio de Strigis*. Unpublished manuscript, Bibliogtheque National, Paris. Quoted in Joseph Hansen, *Quellen und Unterscuchen zur Geschichte des Hexenwahns und der Hexenverfolgung im Mittelalter*, pp.195-200. [1905]. Bonn: Carl Georgi.

as cited in pages 128-131, "The Role of Hallucinogenic Plants in European Witchcraft," from *Hallucinogens and Shamanism*, Michael J. Harner, Oxford University Press, 1973

Page 43
*Lamia*, Keats

Page 44
Dickinson

Page 46-47
Book XI, "Death of Orpheus" from *The Metamorphoses* by Ovid (translated by A.S. Kline)

Page 57
"When the Music's Over" by The Doors


## A SWEET TEEN

Page 67-68
From a popular legend of Bodhidharma.

## ON BATHROOMS

Page 75

Jacques Lacan, trans. Bruce Fink, pg.417, "The Instance of the Letter in the Unconscious," *Ecrits*, Norton, 2007


## ON BEARDS: A MEMOIR OF PASSING

All quoted matter devoid of in-text citation is from *One Thousand Beards: A Cultural History of Facial Hair* by Allen Peterkin, Arsenal Pulp Press, 2001

# ACKNOWLEDGEMENTS

I am grateful to the editors of the following publications in which these pieces first appeared, some in different forms:

"On Bathrooms," *DIAGRAM*; "On Beards: A Memoir of Passing," *Gulf Coast*; "Playing Dead" excerpts, *Seneca Review*; "A Sweet Teen," *Fugue*.

Thanks also to Robert Andrew Perez Jr., Gillian Hammel, and Peter Burghardt of speCt! Books in Oakland, CA for making "On Beards: A Memoir of Passing" into a beautiful letterpress chapbook.

The Research Foundation of the City University of New York (CUNY) gave me time and support through several Professional Staff Congress grants, as did fellowships from the Eugene Lang Foundation and the CUNY Faculty Fellowship Publication Program; I am especially grateful to Shelly Eversley, Bridgett Davis, and Rob Ostrom for support and feedback.

I am incredibly grateful to Kazim Ali, Andrea Abi-Karam, Lindsey Boldt, and Stephen Motika of Nightboat Books. Thanks also to Mary Austin Speaker for designing the cover and interior.

I am most grateful to my queer family; thank you for sustaining me. I am also blessed to have such dear writing kin; thank you, especially, Nathan Hauke and Brenda Sieczkowski.

**ELY SHIPLEY** is the author of *Boy with Flowers,* winner of the Barrow Street Press book prize and the Thom Gunn Award. He teaches at Western Washington University.

## NIGHTBOAT BOOKS

Nightboat Books, a nonprofit organization, seeks to develop audiences for writers whose work resists convention and transcends boundaries. We publish books rich with poignancy, intelligence, and risk. Please visit our website, www.nightboat.org, to learn about our titles and how you can support our future publications.

The following individuals have supported the publication of this book. We thank them for their generosity and commitment to the mission of Nightboat Books:

Elizabeth Motika
Benjamin Taylor

In addition, this book has been made possible, in part, by grants from the National Endowment for the Arts and the New York State Council on the Arts Literature Program.